Professional Soccer Finishing Drills
Top Finishing Drills From The World's Best Soccer Clubs

By Marcus DiBernardo

Table of Contents

1. Long Range Shooting 3v1
2. Long Range Shooting 4v2
3. Liverpool Shooting
4. Long Range Shooting Team Competition
5. Touch Across & Shoot
6. Penalty Box Finishing
7. Long & Narrow Shooting
8. 5v5 Attitude to Shoot
9. Possession and Shooting
10. One-Touch 7v4
11. 3rd Attacker Running & Finishing
12. 3rd Attacker Running & Finishing 1
13. 3rd Attacker Running & Finishing 2
14. Overload Scoring
15. Combination Pattern Shooting
16. 2 Pass Turn and Shoot
17. Barcelona Crossing & Finishing 1
18. Barcelona Crossing & Finishing 2
19. Barcelona Crossing & Finishing 3
20. Crossing and Finishing Pattern Play
21. Red Bull Crossing
22. Finland Crossing
23. Scottish Crossing & Possession

Finishing Drill

Number One & Two

Long Range Shooting 3v1

Grid: 40x36 yards (the penalty box with another on top)
Players: 10

Key Points and Instructions:
The drill is split into 3v1 in each box (4v1 with the keeper). The team of three is limited to two-touch as they try to create space by moving the ball quickly and using the entire area. As soon as a shooting opportunity presents itself they must take it. The lone forward in the opposite box is looking to collect any rebounds and second chances to score. Every shot in this game is from 18 yards and out unless the lone forward steals the ball and shoots. The pace is fast while players get many long range shooting repetitions..

Long Range Shooting 3v1

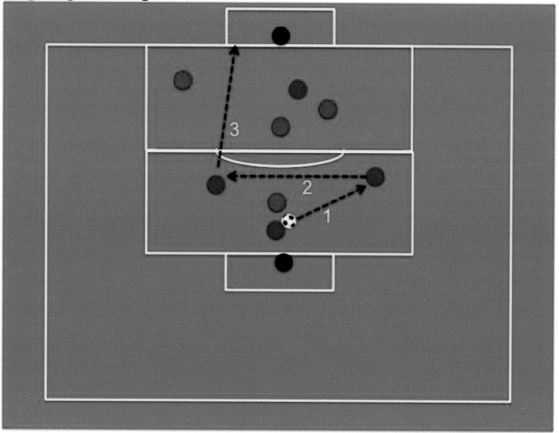

Grid: 40x36 yards (the penalty box with another on top)
Players: 14

Key Points and Instructions:
The drill is split into 4v2 in each box (5v2 with the keeper). The team of four is limited to two-touch. They must create space by moving the ball quickly and using the entire area. As soon as a shooting opportunity presents itself they must take it. The two forwards in the opposite box are looking to collect any rebounds and second chances to score. Every shot in this game is from 18 yards and out unless one of the two forwards steals the ball and shoots. The pace is fast while the players get many long range shooting repetitions.

Long Range Shooting 4v2:

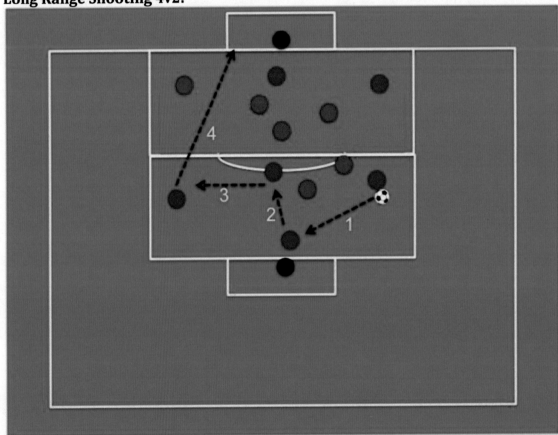

Finishing Drill

Number Three

Liverpool Shooting

Grid: Adjust set-up for the shooting distance desired
Players: 14-23 Players

Key Points and Instructions:

This drill not only provides many shooting repetitions, it also requires accurate passing. The ball is passed firmly to the player's correct receiving foot. The receiving player must play two-touch. Each player follows their pass and moves forward one position. The shooter's first touch should be positive, the second touch pushes the ball by the cone to the side and strike at goal. Placement is the priority. The drill works well if you have a third group stand behind the goals to collect the balls in order to keep the drill moving. After 5 minutes rotate the teams.

Liverpool Shooting:

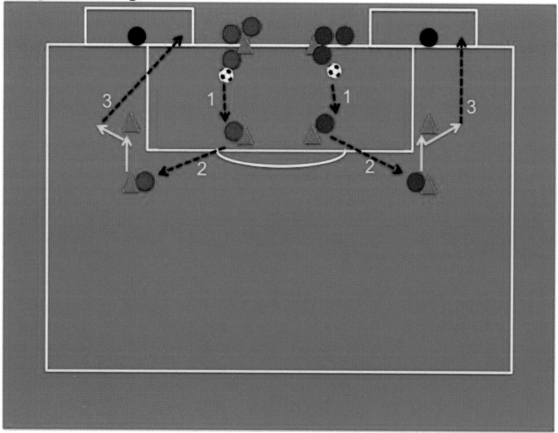

Finishing Drill

Number Four

Long Range Shooting Team Competition

Grid: Adjust set-up for the shooting distance desired
Players: 14-23 Players

Key Points and Instructions:
This long range shooting drill can be modified in many different ways. It provides excellent long range shooting repetitions combined with passing and receiving skills. The ball starts with the end line player who passes it to the middle player. All players follow their pass forward to the next cone. The second player plays into the third for a wall pass. The shooter takes a set-up touch and the second touch is a shot on goal (shot must be taken before the middle line). **Variations:** players dribble through cones before shooting, two teams compete against each other by keeping score (first team to score 10 goals is the winner) Placement is the priority when shooting. .

Long Range Shooting Team Competition:

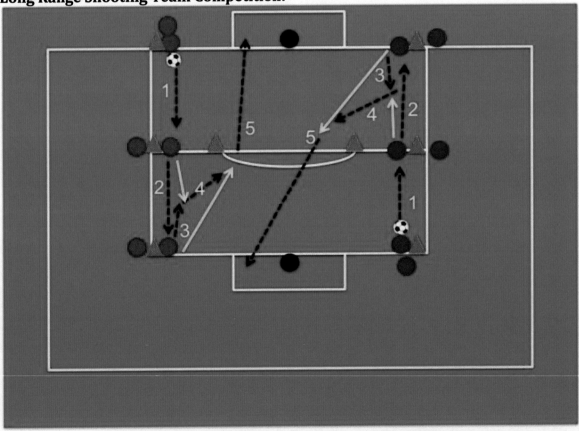

Finishing Drill

Number Five

Touch Across & Shoot

Grid: Penalty Box
Players: 9-12 Players

Key Points and Instructions:
The player runs around the first cone and receives a pass breaking towards the middle cone. The player takes one touch across, moving the ball to the other side of the middle cone and then strikes it. The two lines will rotate every other shot. Focus on placement before power. **Variation to setup:** You can vary the distance of the cones depending on your objective

Touch Across & Shoot:

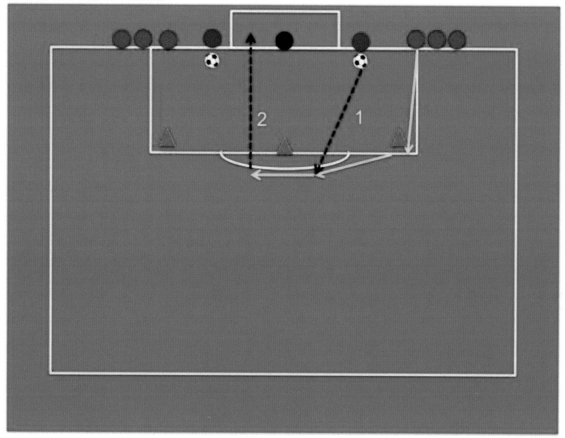

Finishing Drill

Number Six

Penalty Box Finishing

Grid: Penalty Box
Players: 16 Players

Key Points and Instructions:

The penalty box shooting drill involves possession, quick passing, 1-2 combination play and shooting from various angles. Inside the penalty box the blue team will play 5v5 against the red team. The yellow team acts as neutral two-touch players who can't score. The team in possession is trying to score. Once possession is turned over the team in possession must use an outside neutral player before shooting. It is similar to half-court basketball. Players should look for quick 1-2 combinations that will open up shooting angles. One of the reasons I like this exercise is it can be used to teach the players not to panic in front of goal. Possession is a good option in front of goal if no shooting angles are available. Working the ball quickly can produce a chance to score. Forcing a shot or cross because you are in the attacking third is not the right option. After 5 minutes the outside team will switch with one of the inside teams. This training session is from Ajax FC in Holland.

Touch Across & Shoot:

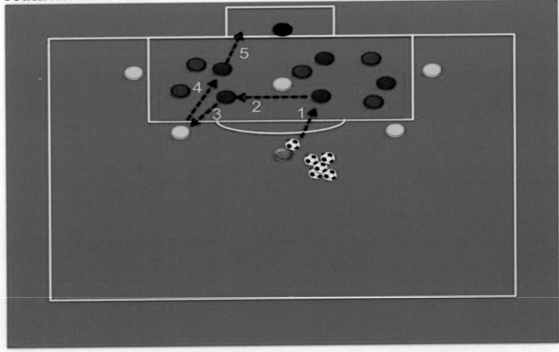

Finishing Drill

Number Seven

Long & Narrow Shooting

Grid: 50x12 yards with 2 Regular Goals
Players: 17 Players

Key Points and Instructions:
5v5 with 6 outside neutral players and 2 keepers (the coach serving the balls in from the outside can operate as a neutral player). The team in possession can score on either goal. If possession is lost, the new team in possession must use an outside neutral player first before scoring. This exercise is similar to exercise number six because it combines possession and shooting in a very tight area. Players should have patience when shooting angles are blocked, quick play, using 1-2 combinations and finding even slight shooting angles to exploit the defense are all key points.
Variations: two-touch restrictions, free play, scoring directly without using outside players.

Long & Narrow Shooting

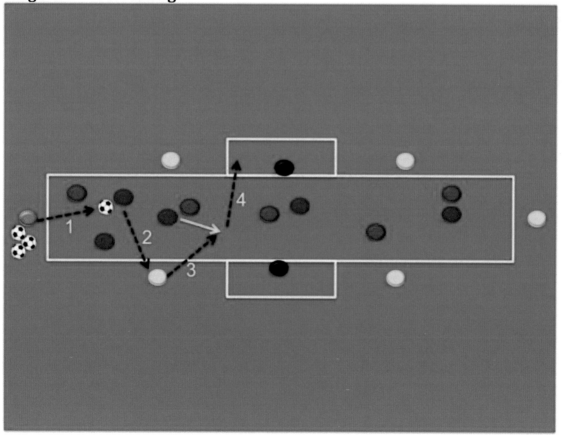

Finishing Drill

Number Eight

5v5 Attitude to Shoot

Grid: 40x36 yards inside field, outside channels 7.5 yards wide, 2 full goals
Players: 16 Players

Key Points and Instructions:

5v5 inside + 2 players for each team placed in the outside channels in the teams attacking half. 2 full sized goals and 2 keepers. This set-up is just like a regular game. Teams are looking to possess the ball with the intention of creating passing angles to shoot. The outside zone players can cross the ball in or play to feet in order to maintain possession. Teams do not have to use the outside players. As soon as a good opportunity to shot arises players should do so. **Variations:** Allow outside zone player to dribble inside creating and overload.

5v5 Attitude To Shoot:

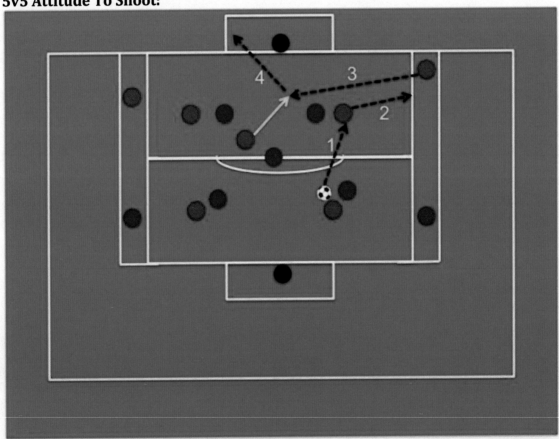

Finishing Drill

Number Nine

Possession and Shooting

Grid: 40x36 yards inside field, outside channels 5 yards wide, 2 full goals
Players: 15 Players

Key Points and Instructions:

6v6 + 1 Neutral and 2 keepers. The red team scores by playing the ball into a side zone to a player running into the zone who stops the ball. When the blue team gains possession they can shoot on either goal for a point. After 5 minutes switch the red team to shooting and blue to possession scoring in the zones. This exercise is another great way to train shooting and possession in a realistic setting. The shooting team must look for opportunities to shoot but also be patient enough not to force chances. The team in possession works on ball circulation with a direction. Variations: remove the neutral player, play 5v5 and limit game to two-touch. This is a training session Brendan Rodgers uses with Liverpool FC.

Possession and Shooting:

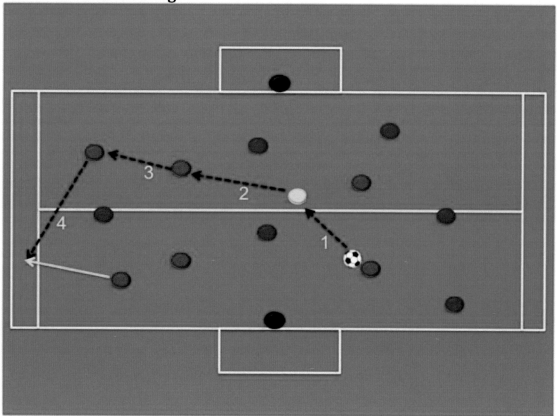

Finishing Drill

Number Ten

One-Touch 7v4

Grid: 40x36 yards (penalty box with another on top)
Players: 12 Players

Key Points and Instructions:
7v4 + keeper. This exercise is mandatory one-touch only. The red team is always in possession of the ball. They must break the 4 defenders down using quick play and coordinated well-timed movements. If the red team loses the ball the game is restarted with the red team in possession again. Offside is played. The blue team must hold the line on top of the penalty box. This exercise is one Jose Mourinho has used with Real Madrid.

One-Touch 7v4:

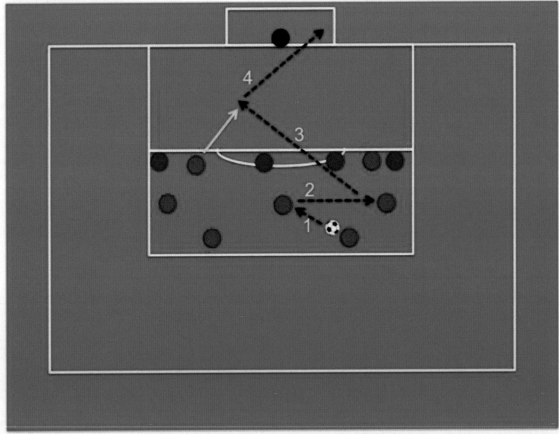

Finishing Drill

Number Eleven & Twelve

3rd Attacker Running & Finishing

Grid: 40x18 yards (penalty box)
Players: 10 Players

Key Points and Instructions:
3v3+3 outside neutrals (who only play for attacking team) + Keeper. The outside players are limited to two-touches. The offside rule applies. The idea is think two or three passes ahead, making use of the 3rd attacker running to break down the defensive line. If the blue team gains possession a new ball is started with the coach on the outside. After 5 minutes reverse teams so each team has a chance to attack.
Variations: Make outside players one-touch, if a defender wins the ball they can take the place of the attacker who gave away possession. This exercise was used by Roberto Martinez at Wigan Athletic FC.

3rd Attacker Running & Finishing 1:

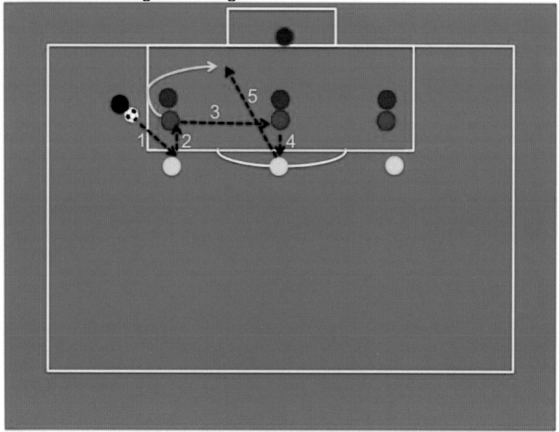

3rd Attacker Running & Finishing 2

Grid: 40x22yards

Players: 10 Players

Key Points and Instructions:

3v3 + keeper. The offside rule applies. The coach serves the ball into the attackers to break down the 3 defenders. The attackers are looking to combine or turn to get off a shot. Players should be trying to think one to three passes ahead. If the defense wins the ball they will try and score on one of the two small goals placed out wide. This exercise was used by Roberto Martinez at Wigan Athletic FC.

3rd Attacker Running & Finishing 2:

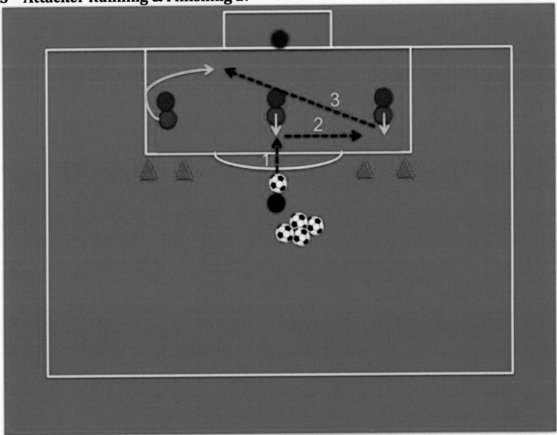

Finishing Drill

Thirteen

Overload Scoring

Grid: 40x36 yards inside field, outside channels 7.5 yards wide, 2 full goals
Players: 20 Players

Key Points and Instructions:

9v9 + Keepers. Both teams have 3 defenders and a keeper in the defensive zone creating a 4v2 overload working the ball out from the back. The midfield zone is 2v2. The attacking zone starts with 2 attackers versus 3 defenders and a keeper. The defenders must get the ball to the midfield zone. The midfielders can play back or out wide to their teammate located in the channel. The ball can't be played out wide from a defender; the ball must be played wide by a midfielder. Once the ball is played wide one midfield player can run into the attacking zone to make it a 3v3.
Variations: Wide player in the channel can dribble inside to make it a 4v3, opposite wide player can join the attacking zone when the ball is passed in by the other wide player making it a 4v3, both wide players can join in making it a 5v3, two-touch for all players, unlimited touch only in the attacking zone. This training exercise is from Stoke City FC.

Overload Scoring:

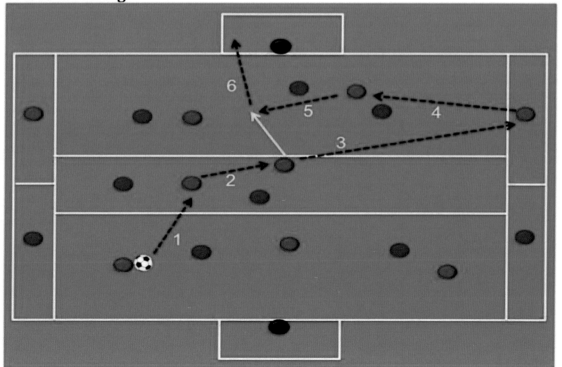

Finishing Drill

Fourteen

Combination Pattern Shooting

Grid: Set-up using penalty box as shown
Players: 10-16 Players

Key Points and Instructions:

Players rotate forward to the next cone after passing with the shooter joining the first cone. Make sure the passing is firm, to the correct foot and eye contact is made. The shooter can finish first time or take a touch to set-up the shot. Placement over power is emphasized. Make sure to have ample balls on hand. If you want to use a third team they can collect the balls as the first two groups are shooting. Rotate teams every 5 minutes. These technical shooting exercises allow players to get numerous meaningful touches on the ball improving their shooting technique.

Combination Pattern Shooting:

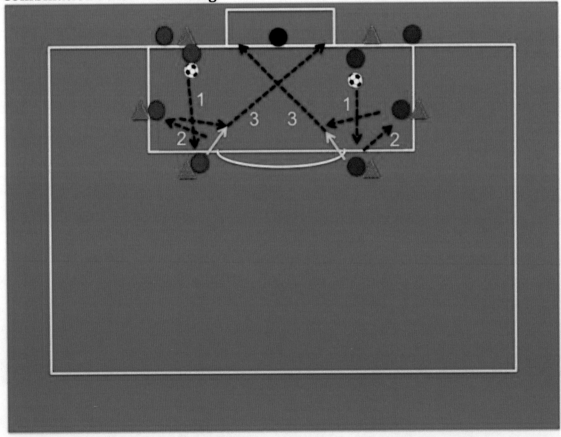

Finishing Drill

Fifteen

2 Pass Turn & Shoot

Grid: Set-up as shown
Players: 9 Players

Key Points and Instructions:

The shooter plays a quick pass in to his partner and receives a pass back to turn one-touch and then finish. The maximum touches the shooter should take would be three including the turn. Keep the balls coming as the groups start in rapid succession one after the other.

2 Pass Turn & Shoot:

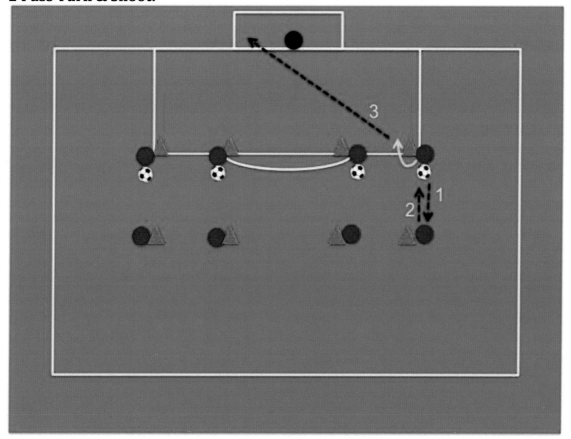

Finishing Drill

Sixteen thru Eighteen

Barcelona Crossing & Finishing

Grid: Set-up on edge of the penalty box extending to the edge of the attacking 1/3
Players: 13 Players

Key Points and Instructions:

This three-part attacking movement involves position specific crossing and finishing. The ball starts from wide with the blue teams right wingback playing the ball into the striker checking back. The striker lays the ball off to the attacking center mid who plays it wide to the winger. The winger is pulling away and back from the outside cone. The cones represent the defensive team's back four. The winger will push the ball to the end line and look to play a cross in on the ground to the near post. The pair of strikers will make their runs into the box. The far striker runs across the box to cover the near post. The other striker stays back on an angle covering the far post. If the near post striker misses the ball or lets it run by the far post striker will finish. The attacking center mid will also make a run central into the box offering another option for the near post runner to flick the ball onto. As soon as the blue team finishes their attacking movement the red team will begin theirs. There should be a rhythm to the pattern with proper timing of runs, firm passing, eye contact and correct foot passing.

Barcelona Crossing & Finishing 1:

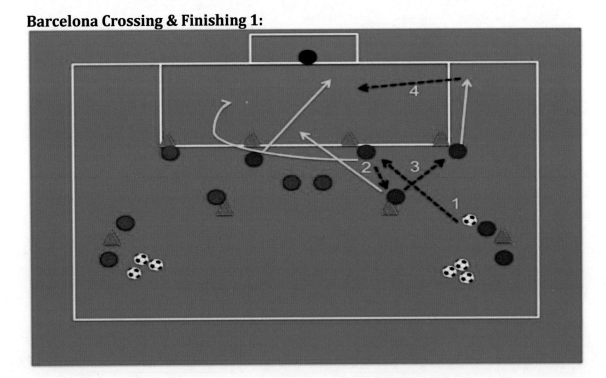

Grid: Set-up on edge of the penalty box extending to the edge of the attacking 1/3
Players: 13 Players

Key Points and Instructions:
The ball starts from wide with the blue teams right wingback playing the ball into the striker checking back. The striker lays the ball off to the attacking center mid who plays it into the winger who is now running inside. The winger will play the ball back to the attacking center mid who will play it out wide to the overlapping outside right wingback. The wingback will take the ball to the end line and whip in the cross to the near post. The pair of strikers will make their runs into the box. The far striker runs across the box to cover the near post. The other striker stays back on an angle covering the far post. If the near post striker misses the ball or lets it run by the far post striker will finish. The attacking center mid will also make a central run into the box offering another option for the near post runner to flick the ball onto. As soon as the blue team finishes their attacking movement the red team will begin theirs. There should be a rhythm to the pattern with proper timing of runs, firm passing, eye contact and correct foot passing.

Barcelona Crossing & Finishing 2:

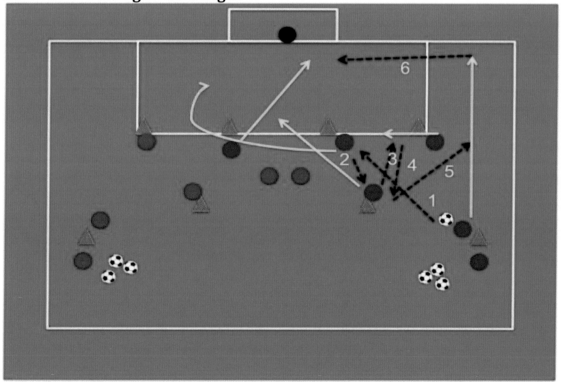

Grid: Set-up on edge of the penalty box extending to the edge of the attacking 1/3
Players: 13 Players

Key Points and Instructions:
The third progression is combination of the first two. The movement pattern is same as the last pattern with the winger making his run inside. The attacking center mid will now have the option to play the ball to the inside running winger or play it out wide to the overlapping right wingback. If the attacking mid plays the ball inside to the inside running winger will allow the ball to run through the back four (cones) and attack goal. The forwards will run into the box and look for winger to pass the ball square for them to finish.

Barcelona Crossing & Finishing 3:

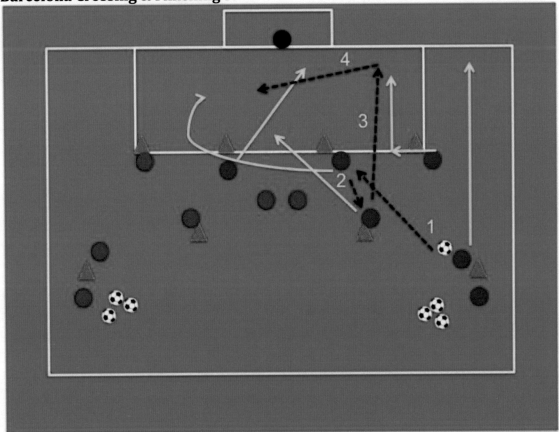

Finishing Drill

Nineteen

Crossing & Finishing Pattern Play

Grid: ½ Field
Players: 12 Players

Key Points and Instructions:

This is a simple finishing and crossing pattern. The blue team will start first. The red team will begin as soon as the blue team shoots on goal. This will allow the timing of the exercise to flow and give the players enough time to get back and ready. Rotate players every 5 minutes. The timing of runs and change of pace in runs is very important. The cross should be seen as an accurate pass to the attacker in the box.

Crossing & Finishing Pattern Play:

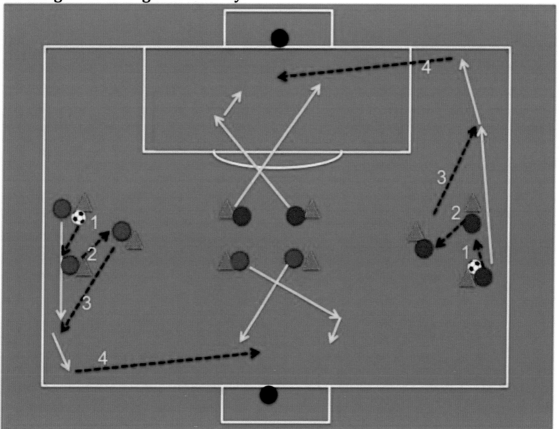

Finishing Drill

Twenty

Red Bull Crossing

Grid: ½ Field
Players: 9 Players

Key Points and Instructions:

This is a simple finishing and crossing pattern. The blue team will start first. The red team will begin as soon as the blue team shoots on goal. This will allow the timing of the exercise to flow and give the players enough time to get back and ready. The timing of runs and change of pace in runs is very important. The cross should be seen as an accurate pass to the attacker in the box. This exercise is used with the NY Red Bulls in the MLS.

Crossing & Finishing Pattern Play:

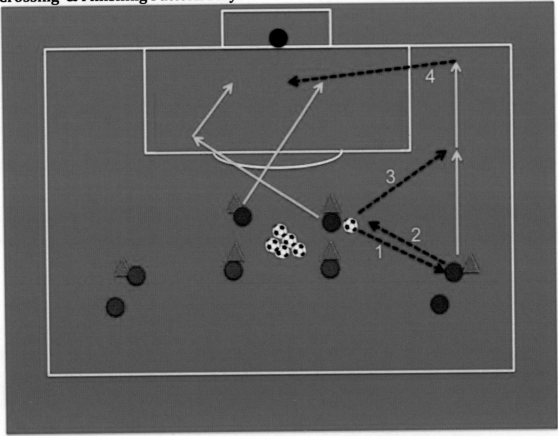

Finishing Drill

Twenty-One

Finland Crossing Pattern

Grid: ½ Field
Players: 9 Players

Key Points and Instructions:

This is a simple finishing and crossing pattern from the Finland National Team. The blue team will start first. The red team will begin as soon as the blue team shoots on goal. This will allow the timing of the exercise to flow and give the players enough time to get back and ready. Both the timing of runs and change of pace in runs ares very important. The cross should be seen as an accurate pass to the attacker in the box.

Finland Crossing & Finishing Pattern Play:

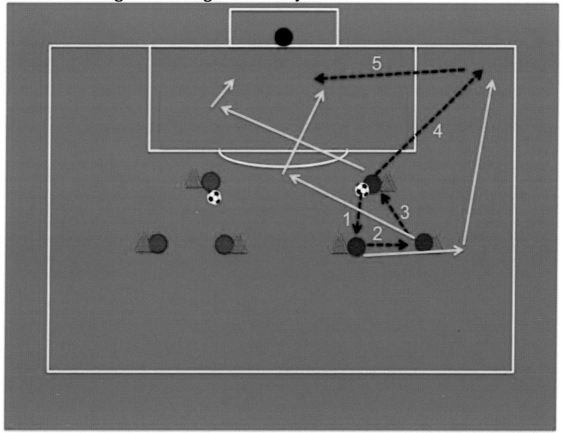

Finishing Drill

Twenty-Two

Scottish Crossing & Possession

Grid: ½ Field, Divided into 3 40x20 yard zones and 2 outside crossing zones
Players: 14 Players

Key Points and Instructions:

4v4 in middle zone. 4 outside crossers (2 for each team) + keepers. Teams play 4v4 in the middle zone looking to connect four passes. After four passes the ball is played out wide to an outside crosser on their team. When the ball is played out wide the player who passed the ball and another will crash the attacking zone looking to for the cross. **Variations:** add a neutral player into the 4v4 middle zone. Reduce the passes to three before the ball can be played out wide. Allow a defender to track back into the box making it a 2v1. Allow 3 players to run into the box and 2 defenders.

Scottish Crossing & Possession:

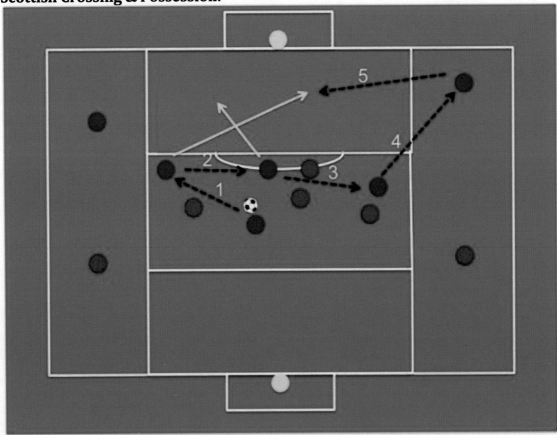

I hope you enjoyed the book. Be sure to check my other titles *"The Method"-The Art of Coaching Soccer, Professional Soccer Passing Patterns, The Science of Rondo, 45 Professional Soccer Possession Drills, The Science of Soccer Team Defending* and more!

Sign up for my email list to receive free drills, articles, information and much more. Email me at coachdibernardo@gmail.com and I will add you to the list.

Made in the USA
Las Vegas, NV
31 December 2024